J 306.481 Lin
Lindeen, Mary,
Playing together /
$22.60   ocn904755866

HARRIS COUNTY PUBLIC LIBRARY

Y0-AVB-688

A Beginning-to-Read Book

Playing Together

by Mary Lindeen

Norwood House Press

DEAR CAREGIVER, The *Beginning to Read—Read and Discover* books provide emergent readers the opportunity to explore the world through nonfiction while building early reading skills. The text integrates both common sight words and content vocabulary. These key words are featured on lists provided at the back of the book to help your child expand his or her sight word recognition, which helps build reading fluency. The content words expand vocabulary and support comprehension.

Nonfiction text is any text that is factual. The Common Core State Standards call for an increase in the amount of informational text reading among students. The Standards aim to promote college and career readiness among students. Preparation for college and career endeavors requires proficiency in reading complex informational texts in a variety of content areas. You can help your child build a foundation by introducing nonfiction early. To further support the CCSS, you will find Reading Reinforcement activities at the back of the book that are aligned to these Standards.

Above all, the most important part of the reading experience is to have fun and enjoy it!

Sincerely,

Shannon Cannon, Ph.D.
Literacy Consultant

Norwood House Press • P.O. Box 316598 • Chicago, Illinois 60631
For more information about Norwood House Press please visit our website at www.norwoodhousepress.com or call 866-565-2900.
© 2016 Norwood House Press. Beginning-to-Read™ is a trademark of Norwood House Press. All rights reserved. No part of this book may be reproduced or utilized in any form or by any means without written permission from the publisher.

Editor: Judy Kentor Schmauss
Designer: Lindaanne Donohoe

Photo Credits:

Shutterstock, cover, 3, 4-5, 6-7 (li jianbing), 8-9, 10-11, 18-19, 20-21, 22-23, 26-27, 28-29; Dreamstime, 1 (© Serrnovik), 12 (© Fotofix); iStock, 13, 14-15, 16-17; Phil Martin, 24, 25

Library of Congress Cataloging-in-Publication Data

Lindeen, Mary.
 Playing together / by Mary Lindeen.
  pages cm. – (A beginning to read book)
 Summary: "Taking turns, working together, and apologizing if you've done something wrong are all parts of playing together. Find out what else you can do to be a good friend. This title includes reading activities and a word list"– Provided by publisher.
 ISBN 978-1-59953-702-3 (library edition : alk. paper)
 ISBN 978-1-60357-787-8 (ebook)
 1. Play–Social aspects–Juvenile literature. 2. Etiquette for children and teenagers–Juvenile literature. I. Title.
 HQ782.L56 2015
 306.4'81–dc23
                                            2015001228

Manufactured in the United States of America in Stevens Point, Wisconsin. 275N-062015

Hi!

Do you want to play?
You can play outside.

You can play together on the swings.

You can take turns pushing and swinging.

5 ...

You can go down the slide.

Your friend can go first.

Then it will be your turn.

Do you want to play catch?

You throw the ball.

Your friend can catch it with a glove.

Good job!

Go up in the tree house!

You can use the ladder.

You can play together up there.

You are up so high!

You can work together.

Look what you did!

Take time to have a snack.

Healthy food will help you grow big and strong.

Do you want to play inside now?

Find something quiet to do.

You can build a house or castle.

You can build other things, too.

What will you make?

Did you make your friend feel mad?

Tell him you are sorry.

Do you see someone who needs a friend?

You can be a friend.

Ask her to play with you.

What fun things do you and your friends do together?

...READING REINFORCEMENT...

CRAFT AND STRUCTURE

To check your child's understanding of this book, recreate the following diagram on a sheet of paper. Read the book with your child, and then help him or her fill in the diagram using what they learned. Work together to identify three important details from the book. Then use those details to tell what this book was about (main idea).

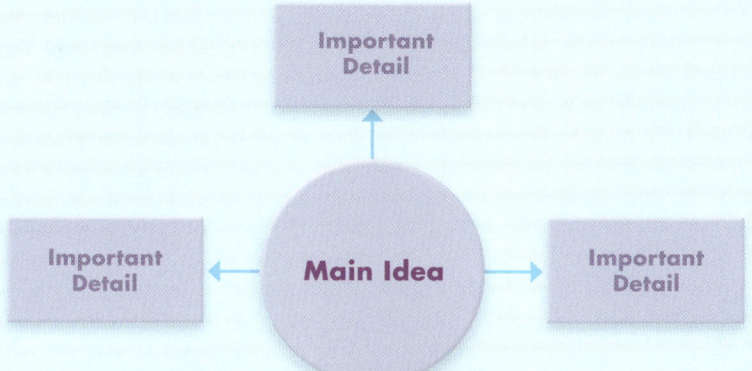

VOCABULARY: Learning Content Words

Content words are words that are specific to a particular topic. All of the content words for this book can be found on page 32. Use some or all of these content words to complete one or more of the following activities:

- Help your child make up sentences that use two or more content words.
- Provide clues about the meaning of a content word, and have your child guess the word.
- Help your child find pictures in magazines that remind him or her of the meaning of a content word. Cut out the pictures. Make a page for a picture dictionary.
- Help your child make up riddles for which content words are the answers.
- Have your child think of synonyms (words with similar meanings) or antonyms (words with opposite meanings) for as many content words as possible.

FOUNDATIONAL SKILLS: Verbs

Verbs are action words. Have your child identify the words that are verbs in the list below. Then help your child find verbs in this book.

| build | pushing | catch | house | job |
| swinging | grow | see | sorry | throw |

CLOSE READING OF NONFICTION TEXT

Close reading helps children comprehend text. It includes reading a text, discussing it with others, and answering questions about it. Use these questions to discuss this book with your child:

- How can two or more people play on a swing set?
- How would you explain taking turns?
- How would you use a ball glove?
- What are the good and bad things about playing with other kids?
- What is a healthy snack that you could share with a friend?
- Why is it important to be a good friend?

FLUENCY

Fluency is the ability to read accurately with speed and expression. Help your child practice fluency by using one or more of the following activities:

- Reread this book to your child at least two times while he or she uses a finger to track each word as you read it.
- Read the first sentence aloud. Then have your child reread the sentence with you. Continue until you have finished this book.
- Ask your child to read aloud the words they know on each page of this book. (Your child will learn additional words with subsequent readings.)
- Have your child practice reading this book several times to improve accuracy, rate, and expression.

••• Word List •••

Playing Together uses the 81 vocabulary words listed below. *High-frequency* words are those words that are used most often in the English language. They are sometimes referred to as sight words because children need to learn to recognize them automatically when they read. *Content words* are any words specific to a particular topic. Regular practice reading these words will enhance your child's ability to read with greater fluency and comprehension.

High-Frequency Words

a	first	look	the	what
and	go	make	then	who
are	good	now	there	will
ask	have	on	things	with
be	help	or	time	work
big	her	other	to	you
can	high	see	together	your
did	him	so	too	
do	house	something	up	
down	in	take	use	
find	it	tell	want	

Content Words

ball	fun	ladder	slide	tree
build	glove	mad	snack	turn(s)
castle	grow	needs	someone	
catch	healthy	outside	sorry	
feel	hi	play	strong	
food	inside	pushing	swing(s, ing)	
friend(s)	job	quiet	throw	

••• About the Author

Mary Lindeen is a writer, editor, parent, and former elementary school teacher. She has written more than 100 books for children and edited many more. She specializes in early literacy instruction and books for young readers, especially nonfiction.

••• About the Advisor

Dr. Shannon Cannon is a teacher educator in the School of Education at UC Davis, where she also earned her Ph.D. in Language, Literacy, and Culture. She serves on the clinical faculty, supervising pre-service teachers and teaching elementary methods courses in reading, effective teaching, and teacher action research.

Harris County Public Library Houston, TX

[5]